For my brother, Ricardo Paul
—BP

For Kevin (Kaiwen), Annika, Daniela, Alejandra, Benn, Minsoo,
and María—and all of my past, present, and future students
—MP

To all my family and friends, who have always supported my dreams;
and for you too, my beloved future reader
—IM

 little bee books

New York, NY
Text copyright © 2018 by Baptiste Paul and Miranda Paul
Illustrations copyright © 2018 by Isabel Muñoz
Manufactured in China   LEO 0423
First Edition
4 6 8 10 9 7 5
ISBN 978-1-4998-0665-6
Library of Congress Cataloging-in-Publication Data
Names: Paul, Baptiste, author. | Paul, Miranda, author. | Muñoz, Isabel, illustrator.
Title: Adventures to School / by Baptiste Paul and Miranda Paul; illustrated by Isabel Muñoz.
Description: First edition. | New York, NY: Little Bee Books, [2018] | Includes bibliographical references.
Identifiers: LCCN 2017023558 | Subjects: LCSH: Education, Primary—Juvenile literature.
Classification: LCC LB1503.P38 2018 | DDC 372—dc23 | LC record available at https://
lccn.loc.gov/2017023558

For more information about special discounts on bulk purchases,
please contact Little Bee Books at sales@littlebeebooks.com.

littlebeebooks.com

ADVENTURES TO SCHOOL

REAL-LIFE JOURNEYS OF STUDENTS
FROM AROUND THE WORLD

BY BAPTISTE PAUL AND MIRANDA PAUL   ILLUSTRATED BY ISABEL MUÑOZ

little bee books

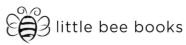

Authors' Note

The scenarios in this book are composites and the narrators' voices are fictionalized, but each is based on one or more real individuals. However, no single child represents all the students in a particular village, region, or country. Each of the nations included have varied landscapes, as well as diverse cultures, peoples, and lifestyles that differ greatly from one home to the next. As we researched, specific students' situations were subject to daily, weekly, or yearly changes depending on climate or politics. And some children choose to go to special, faraway, or boarding schools for reasons such as better opportunities or family preference. But children everywhere still go to school and have the desire to learn about our world and shape the future.

Our hope is that these stories—which capture a few of the most unique, extraordinary, and even dangerous treks—will emphasize the common determination, perseverance, and sense of adventure shared by young people around the world.

Acknowledgments

We would like to thank the many students, parents, friends, travelers, teachers, journalists, and volunteer workers who generously shared their connections, personal experiences, stories, photos, or videos with us. These people include David Sowerwine of VillageTech Solutions, Kshitij Raj Prasai of United Mission to Nepal, Sandhya Sundvor, Kristy and Yutaka Aoki, Jonathan Bing, Melissa Tanke of Working As One, Inc., Salome Ntinyari, Nelson Guda, Noah Sitati, Tuan Le, Vtoàn Ùph, Nadir Sharif, Christian Hendra Limawan, Padma Venkatraman, Aisha Saeed, Lisa Zagar, Andrew Kling and the staff/liaisons at Unbound.org, Per Christian Selmer-Anderssen, Kyrre Lien, Ina Arias Beverley, Kencho Wangmo Dorjee of Snow White Treks and Tours, and Linda LaMie and her students at Angle Inlet School. Any errors or omissions are our own—research was conducted mostly in January–early March 2017.

We also want to thank our editor, Sonali Fry, for leading us to the topic and giving us the opportunity to write this book. A special note of gratitude goes to children's author Margriet Ruurs for a piece of simple advice that allowed us to move forward with our challenging research.

Last, but most important, we wish to recognize students, educators, and educational organizations around the world. Many children whose stories were incorporated into our research expressed a strong desire to get an education. They talked of wanting to shape their own futures and about the individuals who have been working hard to support them in that goal. According to UNICEF, people in many industries are working to change the situation for sixty million children who currently are not going to elementary school, as well as the millions of teenagers unable to attend secondary school. We invite everyone to do their own investigations, find ways to support children who need our attention, and take positive action. We all have a part to play in these stories.

—Baptiste Paul and Miranda Paul

Each day, children around the world face interesting journeys. They have different ways of reaching their destinations, but they're all headed to the same place.

Ustupu, Guna Yala (San Blas Islands), Panama

It's just after midnight when I wake up. There are so many stars in the sky! Nana and Paba pack the canoe with gifts for my host family: plantains, coconuts, bread, chocolate, and coffee. The winter sea is rough and will make the trip last six or more hours.

I slip on a poncho over my *mola* and lie down with a blanket. My parents row while I fall back asleep. After sunrise, I wake up and see land—Ustupu is close! My school is not far from the beach. Nana grabs the food. My host family provides beds for Nana and me so I don't have to make the long trip every day. Paba rests because he will row back home soon. I head straight to school!

Panama is the southernmost country in North America. The mainland rests on a thin strip of land, called an isthmus, between the Atlantic and Pacific Oceans. Cultures and traditions vary, but most Panamanians speak Spanish and are loyal and helpful to their family members.

A unique region along the northern coast of Panama includes hundreds of islands. Several dozen of these islands are home to native peoples such as the Guna (also spelled Kuna or Cuna). Some Guna schools invite students to wear traditional mola dresses on a certain day each week. In Guna culture, the women inherit their father's land, and parents often hope for girls.

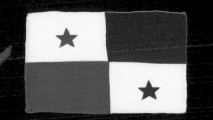

The United States is the world's third-largest country by geographic area. It shares a long border with Canada, the second-largest country by area and record holder of the world's most freshwater lakes. The United States has fifty states—forty-eight of which are connected. The northernmost point of these states is the Northwest Angle in Minnesota, which shares a land border with Canada but not the United States itself.

Americans come from many different backgrounds, and there are 567 federally recognized Native American tribes, communities, and nations in the United States.

Angle Inlet, Minnesota (US–Canada Border)

The thermometer reads -1 °F and it's dark when I leave the fishing house here in Canada. If the ice were thicker, we'd take the truck. But since it's March, we'll take the toboggan. I bundle up in snowpants and tuck my border-crossing card and lunch into my backpack. I help my sisters into the toboggan and put a helmet on. When Grandpa starts the snowmobile, I hold on tight, and we cross the frozen lake in about ten or fifteen minutes.

Today there are a few slush holes and pressure ridges that make the ride bumpy. We park the snowmobile next to the one-room schoolhouse, and Grandpa walks to the special phone to register us with customs. This school in Minnesota is the closest one to us. It's good to be back!

Addis Ababa, Ethiopia

I leave at two o'clock in the morning, Ethiopian time. (In Ethiopia, sunrise is considered 1:00 am.) I carry my baby sister on my back. I don't have shoes, so I step carefully around the garbage piles. I exit through an opening in a metal fence and make sure my baby sister fits through safely. When we reach the busy street, I stay to the side and look both ways before darting across.

I don't make eye contact with security guards or strangers. In the rainy season, I walk through sand and mud where the road isn't paved. Once I reach the footpath into the schoolyard, I can smell the warm breakfast that the staff is preparing!

Ethiopia's mountainous highlands are home to Gelada baboons, a primate that can be found only in Ethiopia. In the northeast desert, an area called the Danakil Depression is one of the hottest, driest, and lowest places on the planet. Fossils from early human history—dating back more than three million years—have been discovered in this area.

Today, most Ethiopians live outside the Danakil Depression region, such as in Addis Ababa, the highest capital city in Africa. Disease, conflict, and famine have orphaned many children over the past decades. Many sibling groups wake up early to do chores or use community washrooms so they can make it to school on time.

More than half of the country's population are Native Bolivians, predominantly Quechua and Aymara. Bolivia is one of the few countries with two capitals—Sucre and La Paz. La Paz, located near Lake Titicaca, is the world's highest capital city. Its neighboring city, El Alto, is the highest metropolitan city in the world.

An electric-powered *teleférico* (with solar-powered Wi-Fi) operates at thirteen thousand feet above sea level, connecting the mountainous cities. It has transported more than forty million passengers since it opened in 2014. Over three thousand students ride the cable car every day at a discounted fare that is the equivalent of less than twenty-five cents.

El Alto and La Paz, Bolivia

Artists are painting a new mural as I enter the station. I walk up many stairs, take out my *tarjeta*, and wait in line. A worker waves me into the moving car. I slide to the far window, and other passengers join me. The doors close, and the busy noise of the city disappears. I feel a little dizzy when the teleférico moves quickly, but the ride is smooth. It's like we're flying! Within minutes, I'm at the stop. I exit carefully onto the yellow strip, then walk downstairs. Just a few more blocks and I'll be at school.

Punjab Province, Pakistan

The rickshaw is so full that all of us can barely fit inside. Legs and arms hang out, and we have to hold on tight. My backpack is tied to the rickshaw so it won't fall. Our driver weaves in between colorful buses, motorcycles, and people. We laugh as we go bump, bump, bump over train tracks and rough patches in the road. By the time I get to school, my hair needs to be combed again!

Pakistan has an ancient history, but it's a relatively new country, formed in 1947. The landscape includes deserts, beaches, and farmland. There are three large mountain ranges, and people live in both villages and cities.

In many families, girls and boys have different roles. Some parents do not send their daughters to school. One famous Pakistani, Malala Yousafzai, was awarded a Nobel Peace Prize for her bravery in standing up for girls' education. At age seventeen, she was the youngest person ever to win a Nobel Prize, but she is not alone in her quest for justice. Her parents, brothers, friends, and many other Pakistani people have been working toward equality.

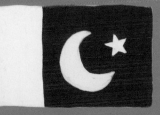

The longest man-made structure in the world is the Great Wall of China. China's climate varies by region, and endangered giant pandas live in remote central provinces.

Lunar New Year, the most popular holiday, falls in January or February. The day before it starts, children are given money in a red envelope, a symbol of luck and good health.

Many families have only one child. When a child loses a lower tooth, they throw it onto the rooftop; and when a child loses an upper tooth, they bury it in the ground. This tradition is thought to help teeth grow straight and in the right direction.

Liangshan Prefecture, Sichuan Province, China

I make sure my shoelaces are knotted well, then walk to the edge of the cliff. My father ties a rope around my little brother. We climb all the way down the heaven ladder. Sometimes I grip the rungs so tightly, I can see the veins in my hands.

We climb down more ladders. Some are loose and need repair. In places where there is no ladder, I hold on to rocks and patches of grass. Farther down, we walk a narrow path to the foot of the mountain. It's a tiring trip, but I won't have to make it again for two weeks. Our school has a place for us to sleep over!

Meru and Samburu, Kenya

I sip my tea and eat my breakfast porridge slowly. I don't want to leave too early, because that could be dangerous. The sun is already warming the land when I join a group of kids with their water jugs and supply bags. We pass by trampled gardens and a damaged house. We see jumbo tracks in the ground. Elephants have been through our village again! We jog for two kilometers in order to reach safety sooner. I'm relieved once we reach school and raise the flag.

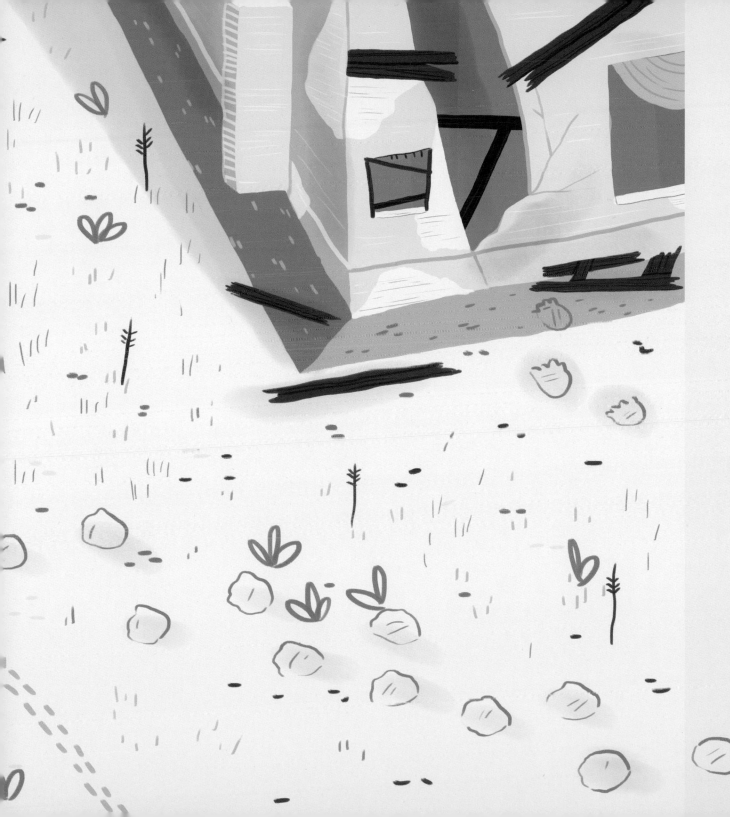

Kenya is a country with towering skyscrapers and mountains, such as Mount Kenya, the second-highest peak in Africa. All of Africa's Big Five animals (lion, leopard, rhino, elephant, and African buffalo) can be found here. Although animals are suffering from loss of habitat and poaching, more than fifty national parks and reserves have been established in Kenya to help keep animals—and the people who live near them—safer.

Yearly, thousands of people from other African countries move to Kenya. Many are in search of a peaceful place to live or a good education. Kenyan students often speak Swahili and English, the two official languages, and at least one of the country's more than eighty local languages.

Nepal is home to yaks, Bengal tigers, elephants, and the world's highest peak—Mount Everest. It is the only country in the world whose flag does not have four sides. Roads are difficult to build in many areas, so some Nepalese people measure walking distances in the time it takes to get there rather than by miles.

Earthquakes, as well as yearly flooding, often wash out bridges, making streams and rivers tough to cross. Despite hardships, some kind of festival is almost always going on in Nepal, including Raksha Bandhan, where sisters tie string bracelets on their brothers' wrists, and brothers give gifts and loving promises to their sisters.

Thumka, Nepal

Above the Trisuli River, a wire bridge will take my brothers, sisters, and me to the other side. They load into the carriage and tuck their books and lunches on their laps and hang on tightly. I tug at the rope. The wheels creak above us. The water below us swells and sprays. My sister gasps, but I remind her the bridge is safer than swimming across the rapids. I sing to calm her. Our voices echo, echo, echo! off the rocks.

Once we reach the far side, I jump out and help push and pull the rope for others. Look at my muscles! When everyone is across, we hike up the hill and walk the rest of the way. If we get to school early, we can chat with our friends before class starts!

Donetsk, Ukraine

I ascend from the basement. Babusya says it's the best place to sleep during the fighting. Now that it's morning, the shelling has stopped. I put on my coat and slip my arm around Grandma. I want to run, but the streets are quiet and Grandma says they're safe to walk on. We hug close to the sides of the tall apartment buildings just in case. After five minutes, I can see the school building. When I get closer, I see teachers cleaning up broken glass. They say everything is all right and welcome us in. Grandma hugs me tight, and I wave goodbye.

Ukraine is the largest country located entirely inside Europe. The landscape is mostly flat, and it is one of the world's leading producers of wheat. In the southwest, where there are mountains, more than a million people enjoy downhill skiing each year.

About 99.7% of Ukrainians can read and write. The people have a strong spirit, having lived through many conflicts and famine. Fighting in the eastern region broke out in early 2014 over a trade agreement. Although subsequent compromises ended much of the violence, some groups continue to fight, threatening the safety of schoolchildren and their families nearby. In the face of this adversity, Ukrainians continue to express themselves with art, literature, music, and dance.

Most Japanese people live in cities. Tokyo is the world's most-populated city with nearly thirty-eight million residents.

Japan's bullet trains, known as *shinkansen*, connect major cities. The thirty-three-mile-long Seikan Tunnel, one of the world's longest underwater railroad tunnels, links the large islands of Honshu and Hokkaido.

Tokyo, Japan

I'm the only one riding the elevator, so I get to push the button. Outside, the traffic is busy, but I'm not worried. I wait for the signal and put my hands in the air. Cute kid crossing here! Then I go—down, down, down into the subway. I slide my pass card through the machine and hop aboard the train. The ride is fast! I count the stops—one, two, three, four.

When I get off, I transfer to another train. I weave in between lots of people, but I wear my yellow flag so grown-ups will help me if I get lost. After one more fast ride, I exit and walk up to the street level. My schoolmates are waiting for me on the sidewalk. We play follow-the-leader inside the school gate. I'm excited to learn new things!

Samdrup Jongkhar, Bhutan

I begin my three-hour walk very early. Although I have my best shoes on, my feet sometimes get hot and blistered. My legs are tired from the journey up steep mountain roads, but I continue. When it rains, my clothes feel heavy and my socks squish. Leeches wiggle around my toes, and the pavement becomes slippery. I must walk carefully, but I don't want to be late. I know that my studies will help me shape my future.

Bhutan is a kingdom that has both a monarch (king) and a prime minister. Its flag features the *Druk*—Thunder Dragon—the country's emblem, which represents violent storms that blow in from the Himalayan mountains.

About 85 percent of Bhutan's land is covered in forests, and almost all the electricity generated comes from hydro-electric (water) power plants. Bhutan became the first country in the world to write specific environmental requirements of its citizens into their constitution.

The majority of children go to school from elementary up to high school.

Cameroon is surrounded by other African countries except on one side, which borders the Atlantic Ocean. The country has a unique shape and location that stretches over lush tropical and montane forests as well as dusty desert. Cameroon Mountain, an active volcano, is the nation's tallest point.

The two official languages are French and English, though more than two hundred different languages and dialects are spoken throughout the country. Adults and students may have to switch languages several times throughout a single day! In some remote villages, seeing a car is rare, but seeing a leopard is even rarer—even though they lurk in both the southern and northern forests.

Bamenda, Northwestern Cameroon

My uncle lifts me up onto his motorbike. I wear a jacket, sunglasses, and a bandanna. These things will help me stay warm and keep the dust from getting in my eyes. My sister rides up front with me. My brothers squeeze in behind my uncle. Our weight slows down the bike, and cars pass us on the straightaways.

Oh no! A tire goes flat. My uncle says he'll fix it. We wait while he finds a shop and some tools. Eventually, we're back on the motorbike and speeding through the busy roundabout. I can't wait to see my friends in the schoolyard today.

Western El Salvador

I wake up early. The air is cool, but the kitchen is warm. I hear oil sizzling and smell fried corn. Yummy *pupusas*! I kiss Mamá and wrap my pupusa in foil. Once I'm dressed and ready, my father leads the horse out front. I brush the horse's mane before we mount him.

Papa and I clip-clop down a deserted path and cross a river in the valley. Once we reach the highway, I still must wait for a bus. My father hands me money for the return trip and waves goodbye. Through the window, I watch him lead our horse back home. My journey is long, but I'm determined. A good education will help me and my family in the future.

More than six million people live in El Salvador, the smallest country in Central America. Since 2001, Salvadorans have been officially using the US dollar to buy goods.

School starts in February and continues well into the year. Almost all Salvadoran students speak Spanish in the classroom. One game that some children enjoy is *arranca cebolla*, where a strong child—the "onion"—holds on to a tree while players link arms and try to pull the onion off.

Look, they've all arrived at school!

PANAMA

US/CANADA

ETHIOPIA

NEPAL

UKRAINE

JAPAN

BOLIVIA

CHINA

KENYA

PAKISTAN

BHUTAN

CAMEROON

EL SALVADOR

How did *you* get to school today?

A Safer Adventure

Several years ago, photos and videos of children around the world making dangerous treks to school became popular on the Internet. People continue to copy and repost these stories without checking to see if they are still current. In many areas, local governments or aid groups have already repaired or built new infrastructure for children who once faced dangerous treks. Those students now have safer journeys to school. The follow-up stories below remind us that not all of what we read on the Internet is complete or up-to-date, and we should always look for multiple sources when doing research.

Karanganyar, Indonesia

Many children walked or rode a bike over rickety planks on an aqueduct bridge. An article published in March 2017 shows a photo of a new, wider, and paved bridge next to the old one.

Los Pinos, Colombia

Children once zoomed down a zipline to cross a 1,300-foot-high gorge to get to school on the other side. According to the headmaster, the school on their side of the canyon reopened in 2015.

Phú Yên Province, Vietnam

During periods of flooding, students tucked their uniforms into plastic bags and waded into cold water, swimming across a river while holding the bags above their heads. Local sources say a boat now comes daily to carry students across.

- Select Bibliography -

Achtenberg, Emily. "Bolivia Revolutionizes Urban Mass Transit: From the Streets to the Sky." Rebel Currents, *The North American Congress on Latin America*. December 26, 2014. nacla.org/blog/2014/12/26/bolivia-revolutionizes-urban-mass-transit-streets-sky.

Adi, Ganug Nugroho. "'Don't Look Down': Braving the Bridge to Get to School." *The Jakarta Post*. April 9, 2014. www.thejakartapost.com/news/2014/04/09/don-t-look-down-braving-bridge-get-school.html.

Aftab, Manik. "'I Fear Travelling in Rickshaws and Vans to School.'" *The Nation*. September 21, 2016. http://nation.com.pk/blogs/21-Sep-2016/i-fear-travelling-in-rickshaws-and-vans-to-school.

Berenson, Tessa. "China: World's Scariest Walk to School." *Time*. May 27, 2016. www.time.com/4350346/china-scary-school-climb-mountain.

Bhutan. The World Factbook. Central Intelligence Agency. January 12, 2017.

Bolivia Guide. Bolivia Facts, National Geographic Society. travel.nationalgeographic.com/travel/countries/bolivia-guide. February 27, 2017.

Brig, and Dan. "Mi Teleferico: La Paz's Cable Car System." *La Paz Life*. February 27, 2017. www.lapazlife.com/the-worlds-highest-cable-car-ride.

"Bullet Train: La Paz, Bolivia, Teleférico Adventure." YouTube video, 3:53. Posted by GIMMENUT, May 5, 2015. www.youtube.com/watch?v=fmpQFi0LKD0.

Burbank, Jon, and Josie Elias. *Nepal*. New York: Marshall Cavendish, 2014.

Cameroon Country Profile. *BBC News*. August 5, 2016.

Cameroon Facts, Cameroon Flag. National Geographic Society. Accessed February 27, 2017.

"Climatic." Tourism Council of Bhutan (Official Website). Accessed February 20, 2017. www.tourism.gov.bt/about-bhutan/climatic.

Craig, Albert M, editor. "Fast Facts: Japan." Scholastic Teachers. 2011. www.scholastic.com/teachers/articles/teaching-content/fast-facts-japan.

Dunbar, Brian. "China's Wall Less Great in View from Space." NASA. Accessed February 27, 2017.

El Salvador Facts, El Salvador Flag. National Geographic Society. Accessed February 27, 2017.

"El Teleférico de La Paz." YouTube video, 2:57. Posted by "DW (Español)," August 11, 2015. www.youtube.com/watch?v=hltpvrHlT-A.

Foley, Erin, Rafiz Hapipi, and Deborah Nevins. *El Salvador*. New York: Cavendish Square, 2016.

Footah, Al, et al. "Panthera Pardus." IUCN Red List of Threatened Species, 2016.

Gish, Steven, Winnie Thay, Zawiah Abdul Latif, and Debbie Nevins. *Ethiopia*. New York: Cavendish Square, 2017.

Gron, Kurt. "Gelada Baboon Theropithecus Gelada." *Primate Info Net Banner*. Ed. Robin Dunbar. September 3, 2008.

Hassig, Susan M., Lynette Quek, and Debbie Nevins. *Panama*. New York: Cavendish Square, 2017.

"Heart-breaking Cliff Ladder: The Most Dangerous School Journey in 'Cliff Village' in China." YouTube video, 4:39. Posted by "Listen to me," May 24, 2016. www.youtube.com/watch?v=ypsEhzjzIhk.

Hogg, George Thomas. "An Introduction to Indian Nations in the United States." National Congress of American Indians. Accessed February 27, 2017. www.ncai.org/about-tribes/indians_101.pdf.

Hoy, Selena. "Why Japanese Kids Can Walk to School Alone." *The Atlantic*. October 2, 2015. www.theatlantic.com/technology/archive/2015/10/why-japanese-kids-can-walk-to-school-alone/408475.

"In Japan, First Graders Travel Solo to School on the Train." *CBS News*. December 15, 2015. www.cbsnews.com/news/japanese-young-children-solo-commute-subway-school.

"Is This the Most Dangerous School Run in the World?" YouTube video, 1:53. Posted by "Barcroft TV," February 17, 2016. www.youtube.com/watch?v=sRNNRahOumU.

"Journey to School." Proloy Chakroborty (blog). June 6, 2013. https://proloy.wordpress.com/2013/06/06/journey-to-school/#jp-carousel-445.

Kent, Deborah. *Ukraine*. New York: Children's, an Imprint of Scholastic, 2015.

Keti, Johnson. "Samburu Residents Say Gov't Considers Elephant Life More Important Than Human Life." *Citizen Digital*. January 12, 2017. https://citizentv.co.ke/news/samburu-residents-say-govt-considers-elephant-life-more-important-than-human-life-154483.

Kuhn, Anthony. "A Harrowing, Mountain-Scaling Commute for Chinese Schoolkids." *NPR*. September 25, 2016. www.npr.org/sections/parallels/2016/09/25/493916854/a-harrowing-mountain-scaling-commute-for-chinese-schoolkids.

Lien, Kyrre. "The School on the Frontline of the War in Ukraine." *Al Jazeera*. August 14, 2016. www.aljazeera.com/indepth/features/2016/07/school-frontline-war-ukraine-160726123423161.html.

National Geographic Society. "Japan Facts." *National Geographic Atlas of the World*, Eighth Edition. Accessed February 27, 2017. travel.nationalgeographic.com/travel/countries/japan-facts.

"No Distance Will Keep Her from School." *Unbound* (blog). September 19, 2016. https://blog.unbound.org/2016/09/no-distance-will-keep-her-from-school/#more-25869.

RAOnline. "Education in Dagana: Community Primary Schools—This Is the Way We Walk to School . . ." *RAOnline Bhutan*. Accessed February 20, 2017. www.raonline.ch/pages/bt/ecdu/bt_edudagana01.html#start.

Rogers, Krista. "Documentary Looks at Why Japanese Parents Let Young Kids Walk to School by Themselves." *Japan Today*. RocketNews24. September 14, 2015. www.japantoday.com/category/lifestyle/view/documentary-looks-at-why-japanese-parents-let-young-kids-walk-to-school-by-themselves.

Ross, Jenna. "Minnesota's Last One-Room Schoolhouse Counts on Its Longtime Teacher." *Star Tribune*. June 1, 2015. www.startribune.com/minnesota-s-last-one-room-schoolhouse-counts-on-its-longtime-teacher/305576541.

Seldon, Pema. "Pre-Primary Education Declines over the Years." *Business Bhutan*. January 2, 2016. www.pressreader.com/bhutan/business-bhutan/20160102/281496455261011.

Sheehan, Sean, and Josie Elias. *Cameroon*. New York: Marshall Cavendish Benchmark, 2011.

Sheehan, Sean, Shahrezad Samiuddin, and Debbie Nevins. *Pakistan*. New York: Cavendish Square, 2015.

Singleton, James. "The Tightly Regulated 'Independence' of Japanese Children." *Nippon*. November 21, 2015. www.nippon.com/en/nipponblog/m00096.

Teklehaimanot, Teum. "Ethiopian Treasures." *Ethiopian Climate and Seasons*. Accessed February 27, 2017.

Thanh, Dang Ngoc, photographer. "Children in Vietnam Risk Lives Crossing River to School." *VietNam Breaking News*. September 24, 2016.

Tshering, Lhapka. "Children's NC Members Question Equity of Central Schools." *Bhutan Times*. January 1, 2017. www.pressreader.com/bhutan/bhutan-times/20170101/281543700596175.

Tucker, Abigail. "Ethiopia's Exotic Monkeys." Smithsonian.com. Smithsonian Institution. December 1, 2009.

UNICEF. "Dangerous Conditions in Ukraine after Heavy Fighting Shuts Down Power, Water—UNICEF." UN News Center. United Nations. February 2, 2017. www.un.org/apps/news/story.asp?NewsID=56092#.WKxQz7YrKi5.

United States. The World Factbook. Central Intelligence Agency. January 12, 2017. www.cia.gov/library/publications/the-world-factbook/geos/us.html.

Urbanc, Cindy Stein. "Lessons from Bhutan." *The Huffington Post*. October 1, 2013. www.huffingtonpost.com/cindy-stein-urbanc/lessons-from-bhutan_b_4027234.html.

Warroad Public Schools. "Angle Inlet School—Warroad Public Schools." Warroad Public School District, 2017. www.warroad.k12.mn.us/cms/One.aspx?portalId=21672625&pageId=23919949.

Yousafzai, Malala. "Nobel Lecture." Nobelprize.org. The Nobel Prize. December 10, 2014.

For a full bibliography, visit www.littlebeebooks.com/books/adventures-to-school